Baking with Ice C
Baking Magic 3: The best ice cream cakes, cookies and desserts recipes

– *A Cake Fairy Cookbook*

by Sabrina Hartford

Summary:

Weave baking magic

Each recipe is thoroughly broken down into easy-to-follow steps, allowing you to effortlessly whip up some truly magical creations, including:
- Pumpkin Ice Cream Pie
- Nougat Meringue Ice Cream Cake
- Neapolitan Banana Split Ice Cream Cake
- Toasted Marshmallow Ice Cream Cake
- Salty Peanut & Pretzel Ice Cream Cake
- Chocolate & Coconut Sorbet Baked Alaska
- Shortbread Honeycomb Ice Cream Cake
- Malted Vanilla Ice Cream Cake
…and many more.

Nutritional information and a full list of ingredients is provided for each recipe.

All recipes are suitable for vegetarians.

Includes 3 FREE additional bonus ice cream recipes!
20 recipes in total + 3 bonus recipes

Contents

3 FREE Bonus Ice Cream Recipes + FREE Future Books

Join my VIP club to get:

1) FREE Cookbook
Ice Cream Magic contains these three bonus ice cream recipes:

BONUS 1:
Cake Batter Ice Cream

BONUS 2:
Pumpkin Ice Cream

BONUS 3:
Lavender Honey Ice Cream

All ice creams can be made at home without the need for an ice cream maker.

2) FREE future books
Selected readers can get some of my future books for free.

3) Discounts and special offers
Get my future books at discounted prices (or even for free).

Use this link to join the club and receive your FREE copy:
http://bit.ly/icecreambook

My club is completely free.

Tips & Tricks

Vanilla

All recipes in this book make reference to vanilla bean pods.

Use the tip of a sharp knife to cut the pod down the seam and then use the same knife to scrape the seeds out. These can then be sprinkled into your dessert for maximum flavor.

Another option is to grind the extracted seeds into a fine powder using a mortar and pestle. You can then mix them into a liquid (such as milk or water) before including them in the dessert.

If you don't have any pods, you can also substitute 1 bean pod with 1 tsp of vanilla extract (although refer to the bottle, as the strength of the extract can vary).

Don't throw away the empty pods: Place them in a sugar jar to add delicious vanilla flavors to your sugar!

Regional Differences

All ingredients in this book are listed by their American names.

Here are the regional equivalents for international readers:
Confectioners' sugar = Icing/powdered sugar
Granulated sugar = Caster sugar
All-purpose flour = Plain flour
Heavy whipping cream = Double cream
Lamington tin = Shallow long cake tin

All measurements are provided in imperial and metric. Unless otherwise stated, measurements list total amounts (So '2 large (30ml) egg yolks' means the total of the two yolks is 30ml). You can substitute regular sized eggs and fruits with large versions (and vice-versa) without any major differences to the taste.

Lemon Meringue Ice Cream Toasted Pecan Crust Pie

Fluffy white lemon meringue and delicious pecan pie are both well-loved treasured classics. This combines both to create a tantalizing treat!

Makes 8 servings.

Ingredients

For the lemon curd
2 large (114g) eggs
2 large (30ml) egg yolks
6 tbsp (85g) unsalted butter
6 tbsp (105ml) lemon juice
2 tsp (3g) grated lemon peel
1 cup (200g) sugar

For the crust
3 cups (¾ quarts, 0.70 liters) vanilla ice cream
¼ cup (55g) butter
1½ cups (160g) chopped pecans
¼ cup (50g) sugar

For the meringue
4 large (120ml) egg whites
¼ tsp (1.5ml) lemon juice
6 tbsp (75g) sugar

Steps

To prepare the lemon curd

1. In a medium bowl, add in the eggs and egg yolks. Whisk until completely combined. Set aside.
2. In a medium saucepan, add in the butter. Cook on medium heat until melted.
3. Reduce to low heat. Add in the lemon juice, lemon peel, and sugar. Whisk until completely combined.
4. Gently whisk in the egg mixture (from step 1).
5. Keep whisking for approximately 8 minutes. When ready, the mixture will become thick. To double check, insert a thermometer into the mixture. The temperature should be approximately 180°F (80°C).
6. Pour the mixture into a small bowl.
7. Cover the bowl with plastic wrap and chill for 4 hours. Do not chill for more than 2 days.

To prepare the crust

1. Leave the ice cream out at room temperature for 10 to 15 minutes to allow it to soften.
2. Preheat oven to 400°F (200°C).
3. In a saucepan, add in the butter. Cook on medium heat until melted.
4. In a bowl, add in the butter, pecans, and sugar. Mix until moist.
5. Place the mixture in a 9″(23cm) diameter glass pie dish. Press the mixture across the base and sides of the dish.
6. Bake for 12 minutes. When ready, the crust will be lightly toasted and will slip down the sides of the dish. Use the back of a spoon to press the crust back into place.
7. Allow the cake dish to cool for 10 minutes on a cooling rack.
8. Freeze for approximately 30 minutes.
9. Divide the ice cream into two halves.
8. Create two layers on top of the crust. The first is a layer of half the ice cream. The second is the lemon curd. Use the back of a spatula each time to ensure the layers are even.
9. Place the dish back in the freezer for approximately 2 hours until firm.

10. Remove from freezer. Use the remaining half of the ice cream to form a new layer. As before, ensure it is spread evenly.
11. Cover the dish and return to freezer for a further 2 hours until firm.

To prepare the meringue

1. Leave the egg whites out so they reach room temperature.
2. In a bowl, add in the egg whites.
3. Mix with an electric mixer on medium until frothy.
4. Add in the lemon juice and mix until completely combined.
5. Continue to mix and gradually add in the sugar.
6. Continue mixing until stiff peaks form.

To assemble the cake

1. Preheat oven to 500°F (260°C).
2. Spread the meringue over the pie, taking care to form a seal at edges.
3. Before serving, bake for 3 minutes, watching carefully to ensure that it doesn't burn. When ready, golden patches will form on the meringue.
4. Serve while warm for the best taste.

Shopping list

Purchase specialty ingredients on Amazon:

Pecan nuts: http://amzn.to/2HG29v8

Nutritional information (per serving)

Calories	491	
Total Fat	32.9g	(daily value 42%)
Saturated Fat	12.1g	(daily value 60%)
Trans Fat	0.233g	
Cholesterol	180mg	(daily value 60%)
Sodium	160mg	(daily value 7%)
Potassium	164mg	(daily value 3%)
Total Carb	46.8g	(daily value 17%)
Dietary Fiber	2.3g	(daily value 8%)
Sugars	44.4g	
Protein	7.3g	
Vitamin A	5%	
Vitamin C	1%	
Vitamin D	23mcg (115%)	
Calcium	46mg (4%)	
Iron	1mg (7%)	

Brownie Ice Cream Cake

An extra-chewy treat made from ice cream with cookie pieces, together with a voluptuous helping of cocoa powder for an unbeatable chocolate taste!

Makes 12 servings.

Ingredients

For the brownie and filling
4 cups (1 quart, 1 liter) cookies ice cream
½ cup (115g) butter
1 cup (200g) white sugar
1 vanilla bean
½ cup (60g) all-purpose flour
¼ tsp (1.2g) baking powder
⅓ cup (40g) unsweetened cocoa powder
¼ tsp (1.5g) salt
3 large (171g) eggs
½ cup (120ml) oil
¼ cup (60ml) water

For the frosting
2 cups (480g) heavy whipping cream
1 cup (125g) confectioners' sugar
½ tsp (1.5g) salt

Steps

To prepare the brownie and filling
1. Leave the ice cream out at room temperature for 10 to 15 minutes to allow it to soften.
2. Preheat oven to 350°F (180°C).

3. In a large saucepan, add in the butter. Cook on medium heat until melted.
4. Remove from heat. Add in the sugar and vanilla while stirring.
5. Add in the all-purpose flour, baking powder, cocoa, and salt. Mix until completely combined.
6. Add in the eggs, oil, and water. Mix until combined.
7. Spray two 10″ (25.5cm) cake tins with a small amount of nonstick cooking spray. Pour mixture into tins.
8. Bake for 20 minutes.
9. Allow to completely cool. Then remove from tin and place on a plate.
10. Scoop the ice cream onto the first brownie. Take care to ensure the scoops are of an even size.
11. Place the second brownie on top and slightly press down.
12. Place into freezer for approximately 3 hours to set.

To prepare the frosting
1. In a bowl, add in the cream. Mix with an electric mixer until stiff peaks form.
2. Add in the confectioners' sugar and salt.

To finish the cake
1. Remove cake from freezer.
2. Spread the frosting over the cake. Use the back of a spatula to create a smooth and even layer.
3. Freeze for a further 10 minutes before serving.

Shopping list

Purchase specialty ingredients on Amazon:

Cookies ice cream: http://amzn.to/2p81xqd

Unsweetened cocoa powder: http://amzn.to/2FxB9Bd

Nutritional information (per serving)

Calories	346	
Total Fat	24.7g	(daily value 32%)
Saturated Fat	10.3g	(daily value 51%)
Trans Fat	0.358g	
Cholesterol	102mg	(daily value 34%)
Sodium	156mg	(daily value 7%)
Potassium	85mg	(daily value 5%)
Total Carb	30.1g	(daily value 11%)
Dietary Fiber	1.3g	(daily value 4%)
Sugars	23.9g	
Protein	4.5g	
Vitamin A	3%	
Vitamin C	1%	
Vitamin D	10mcg (49%)	
Calcium	68mg (5%)	
Iron	1mg (6%)	

Chocolate Salted Caramel Ice Cream Cake

Salt flakes in a dessert is certainly unusual. However, the flakes compliment both the caramel syrup and vanilla ice cream, resulting in an interesting treat that stimulates all the taste buds!

Makes 12 servings.

Ingredients

For the crust and cookie crumbs
18 chocolate graham crackers (3.2oz, 94.5g)
1 tsp (6g) salt
¼ cup (50g) granulated sugar
¾ cup (170g) unsalted butter

For the ganache
1¼ cups (295ml) heavy cream
2 cups (340g) semisweet chocolate chips

For the salted caramel
1 tbsp (15ml) light corn syrup
1 cup (200g) sugar
¼ cup (55g) unsalted butter
½ cup (120ml) heavy cream
¾ tsp (4.5g) salt
1 vanilla bean

For the assembly
38 cups (9½ quarts, 9 liters) vanilla ice cream

For when ready to serve
2 tsp (12g) flake salt

Steps

To prepare the crust and cookie crumbs
1. In a food processor, add in the graham crackers. Blend to create crumbs.
2. In a medium bowl, add in the crumbs, salt, and sugar. Mix until completely combined. Set aside.
3. In a saucepan, add in the butter. Cook on medium heat until melted stirring regularly.
4. Pour the melted butter in the bowl of dry ingredients (from step 2). Mix until crumbs are completely moistened.
5. Divide the crumbs mixture into two halves.
6. Spray a 9"(23cm) springform tin with cooking spray. Pour the first half of the crumbs mixture into the tin. Press down ensuring it forms an even layer on the base. It should also form a 1"(2.5cm) high crust on the sides.
7. Line a baking sheet with baking paper. Spread the second half of the crumbs mixture on to the baking sheet.
8. Place the tin and baking sheet into a freezer for at least 30 minutes.

To prepare the ganache
1. In a medium saucepan, add in the heavy cream. Cook on medium heat until it just begins to bubble.
2. Remove from heat and immediately add in the chocolate chips. Mix until the chips are completely melted. The final mixture should be shiny and smooth.

To prepare the salted caramel
1. In a saucepan, add in the corn syrup and sugar.
2. Cook on medium heat and swirl until the sugar melts (Avoid stirring. But if it is necessary to make the sugar melt, then stir very gently).
3. When the sugar begins to turn amber, remove from heat.
4. Immediately add in the butter and heavy cream. Take care when doing so as it could bubble up and rapidly foam. After adding the ingredients, quickly stir until all is completely combined.

5. Return to medium heat. Continue cooking until the shade becomes darker. Take care while cooking as it can quickly turn black, which won't taste nice.
6. Remove from heat.
7. Add in the salt and vanilla. Stir until completely combined.
8. Allow to cool to room temperature.

To assemble the cake

1. Remove the crust from the freezer.
2. Divide the ganache into two halves. Place one half on top of the cake. Use the back of a spatula to create a smooth and even layer. Return to freezer for approximately 30 minutes.
3. Remove the crust again from freezer. Divide the ice cream into two halves. Place the first half of the ice cream on top, again taking care to create a smooth and even layer. There should be no gaps or air bubbles. As before, return to freezer for a further 30 minutes.
4. Remove both the tin and baking sheet from freezer. Pour two-thirds of the crumbs over the ice cream layer. Then pour three-quarters of the salted caramel over the crumbs. Return to freezer for a further 30 minutes.
5. Remove cake from freezer again and place the remaining ice cream on top. As before, create a smooth layer that is free of gaps and bubbles. Re-freeze for 30 minutes.
6. Remove cake from freezer. Now create the following layers: remaining ganache, remaining crumbs, remaining caramel. Ensure each layer is smooth. Return to freezer for 1 hour.

To serve

1. Dip a large knife into boiling water. Run around the inside edge of the cake tin to loosen the cake.
2. Remove cake from tin.
3. Sprinkle the flake salt on top.

Shopping list

Purchase specialty ingredients on Amazon:

Graham crackers:	http://amzn.to/2FInAy7
Semisweet chocolate chips:	http://amzn.to/2p8z2Jc
Flake salt:	http://amzn.to/2FydqAM

Nutritional information (per serving)

Calories	652	
Total Fat	42.9g	(daily value 55%)
Saturated Fat	26.7g	(daily value 134%)
Trans Fat	0.012g	
Cholesterol	101mg	(daily value 34%)
Sodium	390mg	(daily value 17%)
Potassium	173mg	(daily value 4%)
Total Carb	67g	(daily value 24%)
Dietary Fiber	2.5g	(daily value 9%)
Sugars	54.5g	
Protein	3.8g	
Vitamin A	5%	
Vitamin C	0%	
Vitamin D	27mcg (133%)	
Calcium	99mg (8%)	
Iron	1mg (4%)	

Pumpkin Ice Cream Pie

A rich melody of flavors consisting of crushed gingersnap cookies, maple syrup, pumpkin bread and of course pumpkin ice cream.

Makes 8 servings.

Ingredients

For the cake
6 tbsp (85g) butter
2 cups (200g) crushed gingersnap cookies
1 tbsp (12g) brown sugar

For the filling
2 tbsp (25g) brown sugar
1 cup (240g) heavy whipping cream
1 tbsp (15ml) maple syrup
2 vanilla beans

For the assembly
4 cups (1 quart, 1 liter) pumpkin ice cream*
2 cups (200g) crumbled pumpkin bread
½ cup (55g) chopped pecan nuts

A recipe to make this at home is in included in your free bonus book. See end of this book for details.

Steps

To prepare the cake

1. In a saucepan, add in the butter. Cook on low heat until melted.
2. In a large bowl, add in the gingersnaps, brown sugar, and melted butter. Mix until completely combined.
3. Spray a 9″(23cm) pie tin with nonstick cooking spray.
4. Press mixture against pie tin. Freeze for 30 minutes.

To prepare the filling

1. Place a metal bowl in a fridge to allow it to chill. Then remove from fridge and add in the brown sugar, heavy whipping cream, maple syrup, and vanilla.
2. Beat until medium stiff peaks form.
3. Refrigerate for at least 30 minutes.

To assemble the cake

1. Leave the ice cream out at room temperature for 10 to 15 minutes to allow it to soften.
2. Remove pie from freezer. Spread ice cream on pie. Use the back of a spatula to create a smooth and even layer.
3. Top with crumbled pumpkin bread and then with the filling. Freeze for at least 2 hours.
4. Sprinkle pecan nuts on top.

Shopping list

Purchase specialty ingredients on Amazon:

Gingersnap cookies: http://amzn.to/2FPvouQ

Maple syrup: http://amzn.to/2FJCHbi

Pumpkin ice cream
(not always available):   http://amzn.to/2G4ua22

Pumpkin bread: http://amzn.to/2HHkyYt

Pecan nuts: http://amzn.to/2HG29v8

Nutritional information (per serving)

Calories	439	
Total Fat	28.8g	(daily value 37%)
Saturated Fat	14g	(daily value 70%)
Trans Fat	0.361g	
Cholesterol	76mg	(daily value 25%)
Sodium	315mg	(daily value 14%)
Potassium	120mg	(daily value 3%)
Total Carb	40.8g	(daily value 15%)
Dietary Fiber	1.4g	(daily value 5%)
Sugars	20.5g	
Protein	3.6g	
Vitamin A	31%	
Vitamin C	1%	
Vitamin D	6mcg (30%)	
Calcium	98mg (8%)	
Iron	2mg (11%)	

Nougat Meringue Ice Cream Cake

Chewy sweet nougat, a delicious meringue, and extra helpings of ice cream and nuts create an irresistible experience that is simultaneously soft, fluffy, and crunchy!

Makes 12 servings.

Ingredients

For the three meringue layers
6 regular (180ml) egg whites
½ tsp (3ml) lemon juice
2 cups (480g) granulated sugar

For the filling
25 cups (6 quarts, 1 liter) vanilla ice cream
2 cups (300g) chopped macadamia nougat

For when ready to serve
2 cups (500ml) fresh cream†
7oz (200g) dark chocolate
Handful of blueberries for decoration*
Handful of strawberries for decoration*

†*Fresh cream contains 25% fat. You can use heavy whipping cream, although as this normally contains 35% fat, the finish won't be as light.*

Vary amount according to preference.

Steps

To prepare the three meringue layers

1. Preheat the oven to 320°F (160°C).
2. In a bowl, add in the egg whites and lemon juice. Beat until very stiff.
3. In a food processor, add in the sugar. Blend for approximately 3 minutes until superfine.
4. Separate the sugar into eight 1 tbsp (12g) servings. Gradually add in each spoonful into the egg whites mixture, mixing well after each. Fold in the remaining sugar, mixing to ensure it is evenly distributed. Take care not to over mix.
5. Pour the mixture into a piping bag that has a 0.4" (1cm) piping tip.
6. Line a baking tray with baking paper. With a pen draw three 10" (25cm) diameter circles to act as a guide.
7. Pipe the meringue using a coil-like maneuver onto the three circles.
8. Bake for approximately 35 minutes. When ready it will become a pale golden brown color, but the center will remain slightly soft without turning dry.
9. Remove tray from oven and allow to cool.

To prepare the filling

1. Leave the ice cream out at room temperature for 10 to 15 minutes to allow it to soften.
2. In a bowl, add in the ice cream and nougat. Mix until softened.
3. Divide the mixture into two halves. Set aside.

To assemble the cake

1. Cut a circle shape from baking paper. The size should be the same as the meringues (10″ or 25 cm). Line the base of a springform cake tin with paper, then place the first meringue on top.
2. Create a layer on top of the meringue using the first half of the ice cream mixture (from step 3 of the filling preparation). Then place the second meringue on top. Repeat this step to use the remaining ice cream mixture and meringue. On each attempt use the back of a spatula to create a smooth and even layer of ice cream. Once finished, freeze for 8 hours.

To serve

1. When ready to serve, remove cake from tin and turn upside down.
2. In a bowl, add in the fresh cream. Whip until thick.
3. Top the cake with cream. Grate the chocolate on top and then add the blueberries and strawberries.

Shopping list

Purchase specialty ingredients on Amazon:

Macadamia nougat	http://amzn.to/2u5eelk
Dark chocolate	http://amzn.to/2lAbRAr
Blueberries	http://amzn.to/2pnfCRF
Strawberries	http://amzn.to/2G41lTl

Steps

General preparation
Leave all ice creams out at room temperature for 30 minutes to allow them to soften.

For the crust
1. Preheat oven to 350°F (180°C).
2. In a medium-sized saucepan, add in the butter. Cook on low heat until it has melted.
3. Remove from heat and allow to cool slightly.
4. Once cooled, pour the melted butter into a food processor. Add in the crushed wafers and blend until completely combined.
5. Pour the mixture into a springform tin. Press it down so it covers 1″ (2.5cm) of the bottom and sides.
6. Bake in oven for approximately 10 to 20 minutes to help the crumbs form a more solid crust. Keep checking after the first 10 minutes to ensure the crust doesn't burn. Remove from oven. Allow to completely cool.

For the first layer
1. In a large bowl, add in the chocolate ice cream and mix with an electric mixer until all the fluffiness has gone and the mixture is uniformly creamy (You can do it by hand, but it will take longer).
2. Pour into the springform tin until it forms a 1″(2.5cm) deep layer over the crust. Use the back of a spatula to create a smooth and even layer.

For the second, third, and fourth layers
1. Cut the chocolate bars into small chunks.
2. In a bowl, add in the chocolate bar chunks and the crushed cookies.
3. Mix until completely combined.
4. As before, pour the mixture to create a layer. Use the back of a spatula to make it smooth and even.
5. Place into freezer for approximately 1 hour.

6. Repeat steps 4 and 5 for the fudge sauce and then the vanilla ice cream. Take care to ensure all layers are smooth and have been kept in the freezer for 1 hour before moving on to the next layer. When adding the vanilla ice cream, pour enough so the layer leaves a ½"(1.30cm) gap from the top of the springform tin.

For the fifth layer

1. Leave the whipped topping out at room temperature to allow it to soften.
2. Remove the springform tin from the freezer.
3. Spread the defrosted whipped topping to form a ½" (1.30cm) layer.
4. Sprinkle the chopped nuts on top.
5. Freeze for a further 4 hours until firm.

To serve

1. Remove the cake from the freezer 20 minutes before serving.
2. Dip a large knife into boiling water. Run around the inside edge of the cake tin to loosen the cake.
3. Release the side wall of the springform tin. Cut the cake into wedges. Dip a knife into boiling water before cutting each slice to make it easier.

Shopping list

Purchase specialty ingredients on Amazon:

Wafers	http://amzn.to/2GHE1Jj
Chocolate ice cream	http://amzn.to/2tZzJKv
Fudge sauce	http://amzn.to/2FMZjrK
Vanilla ice cream	http://amzn.to/2IxNJ1g
Frozen whipped topping	http://amzn.to/2FUAo1t
Nuts	http://amzn.to/2G7LP98

Nutritional information (per serving)

Calories	555	
Total Fat	32g	(daily value 41%)
Saturated Fat	16.7g	(daily value 83%)
Trans Fat	0.186g	
Cholesterol	57mg	(daily value 19%)
Sodium	297mg	(daily value 13%)
Potassium	282mg	(daily value 6%)
Total Carb	62.2g	(daily value 23%)
Dietary Fiber	2.7g	(daily value 10%)
Sugars	39.3g	
Protein	7.2g	
Vitamin A	1%	
Vitamin C	17%	
Vitamin D	3mcg (16%)	
Calcium	115mg (9%)	
Iron	2mg (14%)	

Neapolitan Banana Split Ice Cream Cake

A wonderful twist on the classic banana split that uses a cake instead of a split banana. It also includes Neapolitan ice creams to further create an original and inventive taste.

Makes 8 servings.

Ingredients

For the base cake

1½ cups (½ quart, 0.35 liters) chocolate ice cream
1 cup (¼ quart, 0.25 liters) strawberry ice cream
1 cup (¼ quart, 0.25 liters) vanilla ice cream
2½ cups (250g) chocolate cookie crumbs
2 medium ripe bananas, cut into ¼" (0.6cm) circles

For the finishing

½ cup (150g) fudge sauce
1 cup (240ml) whipped cream

Steps

To prepare the base cake

1. Leave the 3 ice creams out at room temperature for 10 to 15 minutes to allow them to soften.
2. Line a 9" (23cm) cake tin with plastic wrap. Ensure there is an overhang on both sides.
3. Add in the chocolate ice cream. Use the back of a spatula to spread it out into an even layer.
4. Divide the cookie crumbs into thirds. Spread the first third on top of the chocolate ice cream to form an even layer.
5. Now create the following layers: vanilla ice cream, an additional layer of crumbs, banana slices, strawberry ice

cream, final third of cookie crumbs. Ensure each layer is smooth.
6. Chill for 4 hours to harden. Do not leave for longer than 8 hours, or it will become too hard.

To finish the cake
1. Remove from freezer.
2. Gently lift the plastic wrap to ease the cake out. If it doesn't release, then dip a large knife into boiling water. Run around the inside edge of the cake tin to loosen the cake.
3. Warm the fudge sauce until hot. Then spread over cake.
4. Top with cream before serving.

Shopping list

Purchase specialty ingredients on Amazon:

Chocolate ice cream	http://amzn.to/2G5JFGY
Strawberry ice cream	http://amzn.to/2FLLdXt
Vanilla ice cream	http://amzn.to/2G5n917
Fudge sauce	http://amzn.to/2FMZjrK
Whipped cream	http://amzn.to/2u1QHba

Nutritional information (per serving)

Calories	268	
Total Fat	14.8g	(daily value 19%)
Saturated Fat	7.8g	(daily value 39%)
Trans Fat	0.1g	
Cholesterol	38mg	(daily value 13%)
Sodium	199mg	(daily value 9%)
Potassium	217mg	(daily value 5%)
Total Carb	32.3g	(daily value 12%)
Dietary Fiber	1.9g	(daily value 7%)
Sugars	14.7g	
Protein	3.3g	
Vitamin A	8%	
Vitamin C	10%	
Vitamin D	0mcg (0%)	
Calcium	42mg (3%)	
Iron	1mg (7%)	

Ice Cream Chocolate Chip Cookies

These look like regular cookies but have the secret ingredient of ice cream inside! They can be made with any flavor of ice cream and won't fail to bring a welcome surprise to all who taste them!

Makes 24 cookies.

Ingredients

½ cup (110g) unsalted butter
½ cup (100g) light brown sugar, packed
⅓ cup (65g) granulated sugar
½ cup (0.12 liters) ice cream (any flavor)
1 large (57g) egg
1 vanilla bean
½ tsp (2.4g) baking soda
¼ tsp (1.5g) salt
2 cups (250g) all-purpose flour
2 cups (350g) chocolate chips

Steps

1. In a saucepan, add in the butter. Cook on medium heat until melted.
2. In a bowl, add in the melted butter while still hot, together with both sugars. Mix using an electric mixer until completely combined.
3. Add in the ice cream and continue mixing until smooth.
4. Add in egg and vanilla. Mix for 5 seconds.
5. Add in the baking soda and salt. Mix until smooth.
6. Reduce the mixer to a slow speed and gently add in the all-purpose flour while mixing. Continue mixing until just combined.
7. Add in the chocolate chips and gently stir to distribute them.
8. Line a cookie sheet with baking paper.

9. Scoop the dough into a ball shape. Each ball will need 2 tablespoons of the dough (approx. 2g although vary amount to form a solid cookie shape). Place on the cookie sheet leaving a 2″ (5cm) space between each one.
10. Cover with plastic wrap. Refrigerate for a minimum of 1 hour.
11. Preheat oven to 350°F (180°C).
12. Remove plastic wrap and transfer cookies to the oven. (If you have chilled them for too long, you may need to press them down slightly to ensure they properly flatten).
13. Bake for approximately 10 minutes. When ready, the edges will become golden. Keep checking after the first 8 minutes to ensure they don't burn.
14. Allow to cool for 5 minutes on the cookie sheet.
15. Remove cookies and place on a cooling rack until fully cooled.

Storage
Either keep the cookies frozen for up to 3 weeks or store in an airtight container for up to 3 days.

Shopping list
Purchase specialty ingredients on Amazon:

Ice cream   http://amzn.to/2G7xj1h

Chocolate chips   http://amzn.to/2FTi8VT

Nutritional information (per serving)

Calories	181	
Total Fat	8.5g	(daily value 11%)
Saturated Fat	5.6g	(daily value 28%)
Trans Fat	0g	
Cholesterol	22mg	(daily value 7%)
Sodium	94mg	(daily value 4%)
Potassium	78mg	(daily value 2%)
Total Carb	23.8g	(daily value 9%)
Dietary Fiber	0.8g	(daily value 3%)
Sugars	14.6g	
Protein	2.6g	
Vitamin A	0%	
Vitamin C	4%	
Vitamin D	3mcg (16%)	
Calcium	36mg (3%)	
Iron	1mg (5%)	

Neapolitan Ice Cream Cake Roll

A delicious dessert that combines Neapolitan ice cream flavors (strawberry, chocolate, and vanilla) into a chocolate cake roll, all finished with an irresistible whipped cream frosting.

Makes 8 servings.

Ingredients

For the base cake
¾ cup (90g) all-purpose flour
1 tsp (4.8g) baking powder
¼ cup (25g) unsweetened cocoa powder
¼ tsp (1.5g) salt
3 large (171g) eggs
¾ cup (150g) granulated sugar
2 tsp (10ml) brewed coffee
1 vanilla bean
¼ cup (30g) confectioners' sugar

For the assembly
2 cups (½ quart, ½ liter) strawberry ice cream
1 cup (¼ quart, ¼ liter) vanilla ice cream
1 cup (¼ quart, ¼ liter) chocolate ice cream

For the finishing
Whipped cream for decoration*
Handful of assorted sliced dried fruit for decoration*

Vary amount according to preference.

Steps

To prepare the base cake

1. Preheat oven to 350°F (180°C).
2. In a bowl, add in the all-purpose flour, baking powder, cocoa powder, and salt. Mix until completely combined. Set aside.
3. In a separate bowl, add in the eggs. Beat for 3 minutes at high speed, until frothy and dark yellow. Add in the coffee, sugar, and vanilla. Beat until completely combined.
4. Add in the prepared dry ingredients (from step 2). Mix until just combined.
5. Line a 15.5 x 10.5" (39 x 27cm) jelly roll tin with foil. Then spray with cooking spray and lightly flour. Spread the batter inside the tin. Use the back of a spatula to form a smooth, thin, even layer that reaches all corners of the tin.
6. Bake for approximately 10 minutes. Begin checking the dish after the first 8 minutes of baking as it can burn easily.
7. Place a clean towel on a solid surface. Generously sprinkle the towel with the confectioners' sugar.
8. As soon as the cake has finished baking in the oven, turn it upside down on the towel. Carefully remove the foil.
9. Fold the short end edge of the towel over the cake. Form a tight roll, so the cake is rolled up in the towel.
10. While in the towel, allow to completely cool. Because the towel retains heat, for best results leave overnight.

To assemble the cake

1. Ensuring the cake has fully cooled, take care to unroll it carefully.
2. Leave the 3 ice creams out at room temperature for 10 minutes to allow them to soften.
3. Spread the ice cream to form an even layer on the cake. You want to spread each ice cream flavor so it takes up a third length of the cake. That way, when it is rolled and sliced, each serving will contain all three flavors.
4. Re-roll up again, making a tight roll. Cover with plastic wrap and freeze for a further 5 hours.
5. Remove from freezer. Remove plastic wrap.

To finish the cake

1. Place a layer of whipped cream on top.
2. Decorate with the sliced dried fruit.

Shopping list

Purchase specialty ingredients on Amazon:

Unsweetened cocoa powder	http://amzn.to/2G8MIE2
Brewed coffee	http://amzn.to/2G4mzAB
Chocolate ice cream	http://amzn.to/2G5JFGY
Strawberry ice cream	http://amzn.to/2FLLdXt
Vanilla ice cream	http://amzn.to/2G5n917
Whipped cream	http://amzn.to/2u1QHba
Dried fruit	http://amzn.to/2FI94qW

Nutritional information (per serving)

Calories	170	
Total Fat	3g	(daily value 4%)
Saturated Fat	1.3g	(daily value 7%)
Trans Fat	0g	
Cholesterol	65mg	(daily value 22%)
Sodium	105mg	(daily value 5%)
Potassium	156mg	(daily value 3%)
Total Carb	34g	(daily value 12%)
Dietary Fiber	1.3g	(daily value 5%)
Sugars	20.7g	
Protein	4.1g	
Vitamin A	0%	
Vitamin C	8%	
Vitamin D	6mcg (29%)	
Calcium	51mg (4%)	
Iron	1mg (7%)	

Crunchy Fried Ice Cream Cake

Crushed cornflakes gently fried in butter and then mixed with a generous helping of cinnamon and soft vanilla ice cream... simply amazing!

Makes 12 servings.

Ingredients

4 cups (8oz) whipped topping
7 cups (1¾ quart, 1.6 liters) vanilla ice cream
1 tsp (3g) cinnamon
3 cups (225g) crushed corn flakes (measured after crushing)
½ cup (100g) sugar
½ cup (115g) butter
1 vanilla bean

Steps

1. Allow the whipped topping to thaw.
2. Leave the ice cream out at room temperature for 25 to 30 minutes to allow it to soften.
3. In a bowl, add in the cinnamon, crushed corn flakes, and sugar. Stir until the flakes are completely coated in the sugar and cinnamon. Set aside.
4. In a large skillet, add in the butter.
5. Cook on medium heat until melted.
6. Add in the cornflake mixture (from step 3). Stir constantly for approximately 5 minutes. Take care to ensure the sugar does not burn. When ready, the mixture will be golden brown.
7. Remove from heat and allow to thoroughly cool. Divide into two halves when cool. Set aside.
8. In a large bowl, add in the vanilla ice cream, whipped topping, and vanilla bean. Stir until completely combined. Set aside.
9. Take the first half of the cornflake mixture (from step 7) and spread on the bottom of a 9 x 13″(30 x 20cm) baking tin. Use the back of a spatula to spread it out evenly.

10. Take the ice cream mixture (from step 8) and pour over to create a new layer. As before, ensure layer is even.
11. Take the remaining cornflake mixture and spread to create a final layer.
12. Cover the tin with plastic wrap and then foil. Place in a freezer for at least 4 hours.

Shopping list

Purchase specialty ingredients on Amazon:

Whipped topping http://amzn.to/2HMnovp

Nutritional information (per serving)

Calories	364	
Total Fat	12.8g	(daily value 16%)
Saturated Fat	7.8g	(daily value 39%)
Trans Fat	0.31g	
Cholesterol	35mg	(daily value 12%)
Sodium	212mg	(daily value 9%)
Potassium	630mg	(daily value 13%)
Total Carb	64g	(daily value 23%)
Dietary Fiber	4.8g	(daily value 17%)
Sugars	31.8g	
Protein	3.6g	
Vitamin A	25.9%	
Vitamin C	15.1%	
Vitamin D	27mcg (134%)	
Calcium	656mg (50%)	
Iron	12mg (65%)	

No-Bake Cookie Dough Ice Cream Cake

Milk, cream, and fudge sauce are used to make a chewy cake that is bursting with all kinds of sweetness!

Makes 12 servings.

Ingredients

¾ cup (170g) butter
1½ cups (300g) brown sugar
6 tbsp (90ml) milk
1 tsp (7.5g) salt
2 vanilla beans
1 cup (150g) chocolate chips
3 cups (375g) flour
2 cups (480g) heavy whipping cream
1¾ cups (14oz, 415ml) sweetened condensed milk
½ cup (305g) fudge sauce

Steps

1. Leave the butter out at room temperature to allow it to soften.
2. In a large bowl, add in the butter and brown sugar. Mix until smooth.
3. Add in the milk, salt, and vanilla. Mix until completely combined.
4. Add in the chocolate chips and flour. Mix until a dough forms. (An electric mixer works best, but you can also use your hands.)
5. Line a 9″ (23cm) springform tin with baking paper.
6. Press the dough so it covers the base of the tin and 1½″ (4cm) of the sides to create a crust. Set aside.
7. In a large bowl, add in the cream. Beat until stiff peaks form.
8. Add in the condensed milk. Beat until combined.

9. In a saucepan, gently warm the fudge sauce. Then add to the cream mixture. Mix a few times to allow it to swirl.
10. Pour the cream mixture onto the cookie dough crust (from step 6).
11. Freeze for approximately 6 hours until firm.

Shopping list

Purchase specialty ingredients on Amazon:

Chocolate chips	http://amzn.to/2FTi8VT
Fudge sauce	http://amzn.to/2FMZjrK

Nutritional information (per serving)

Calories	739	
Total Fat	35.8g	(daily value 46%)
Saturated Fat	22.6g	(daily value 113%)
Trans Fat	0.495g	
Cholesterol	107mg	(daily value 36%)
Sodium	401mg	(daily value 17%)
Potassium	317mg	(daily value 5%)
Total Carb	97g	(daily value 35%)
Dietary Fiber	1.9g	(daily value 7%)
Sugars	68.5g	
Protein	9.5g	
Vitamin A	0%	
Vitamin C	8%	
Vitamin D	29mcg (144%)	
Calcium	215mg (17%)	
Iron	3mg (15%)	

ed Marshmallow Ice Cream

Ma__ 'om crushed graham crackers, pecans, and, of course, toasted marshmallows, this is another recipe that manages to be both wonderfully soft and irresistibly crunchy.

Makes 8 servings.

Ingredients

3 tbsp (40g) unsalted butter
8 cups (2 quarts, 2 liters) vanilla ice cream
6 graham crackers (1.4 oz, 42g)
¾ cup (70g) ground pecans
2 tbsp (25g) sugar
¼ cup (75g) chocolate syrup
2 cups (100g) mini marshmallows

Steps

1. Leave the ice cream out at room temperature for 10 to 15 minutes to allow it to soften.
2. In a saucepan, add in the butter. Cook on medium heat until melted.
3. In a food processor, add in the graham crackers. Blend to create crumbs.
4. In a bowl, add the butter, graham cracker crumbs, pecans, and sugar. Mix until completely combined.
5. Pour the mixture into a 9″ (23cm) springform tin. Press it down to form the crust.
6. Drizzle the chocolate syrup on top.
7. Freeze for approximately 15 minutes until firm.
8. Remove from freezer. Spread ice cream on top. Use the back of a spatula to create a smooth and even layer.
9. Return to freezer. Freeze for approximately 2 hours until firm.

10. Remove from freezer. Top with marshmallows. Use a kitchen torch to toast the marshmallows. For best results keep the torch 4″ (10cm) away from the marshmallows. When ready the marshmallows will be puffed and evenly browned. As a substitute for the torch, you can also place the cake in a warm oven, but take care as the rest of the cake will burn or begin to melt quickly.
11. Return to the freezer for 15 minutes.
12. When ready to serve, dip a large knife into boiling water. Run around the inside edge of the cake tin to loosen the cake.

Storage
Freeze for up to 2 days.

Shopping list

Purchase specialty ingredients on Amazon:

Graham crackers   http://amzn.to/2IAQv67

Pecan nuts   http://amzn.to/2HG29v8

Chocolate syrup   http://amzn.to/2G3ccwX

Mini marshmallows   http://amzn.to/2FXgaDW

Nutritional information (per serving)

Calories	238	
Total Fat	13.3g	(daily value 17%)
Saturated Fat	4.5g	(daily value 23%)
Trans Fat	0.006g	
Cholesterol	18mg	(daily value 6%)
Sodium	118mg	(daily value 5%)
Potassium	106mg	(daily value 2%)
Total Carb	28.8g	(daily value 10%)
Dietary Fiber	1.6g	(daily value 6%)
Sugars	18.8g	
Protein	2.5g	
Vitamin A	4%	
Vitamin C	0%	
Vitamin D	3mcg (14%)	
Calcium	31mg (2%)	
Iron	1mg (5%)	

Raspberry & Peach Ice Cream Cake

A beautiful, vibrant cake bursting with wonderful colors and flavors!

Makes 12 servings.

Ingredients

For the fruits

1 ripe peach (approx. 150g)
1 tbsp (12.5g) granulated sugar
2 cups (240g) raspberries
Additional 1 tbsp (12.5g) granulated sugar

For the base cake

5 tbsp (70g) unsalted butter
1 large (57g) egg
1 large (15ml) egg yolk
2 tbsp (30ml) whole milk
¾ cup (95g) all-purpose flour
¾ tsp (3.6g) baking powder
½ tsp (3g) salt
½ cup (100g) granulated sugar
½ vanilla bean

For the cream filling

1½ cups (360ml) heavy cream
½ cup (120ml) evaporated milk
½ cup (155g) peach preserves
Pinch of salt (⅛ tsp, 0.75g)

For the finishing

1 ripe peach (approx. 150g)
½ cup (60g) raspberries
1 tbsp (12.5g) granulated sugar

Steps

To prepare the fruits

1. In a bowl, finely chop the ripe peach. Add in the 1 tbsp of sugar. Set aside for 1 hour to allow ingredients to macerate.
2. Repeat step 1 for the raspberries. However, mash the raspberries instead of chopping.

To prepare the base cake

1. Leave the butter, eggs, yolk, and milk out at room temperature.
2. Preheat oven to 350°F (180°C).
3. In a medium bowl, add in the all-purpose flour, baking powder, and salt. Whisk until completely combined. Set aside.
4. In a separate large bowl, add in the butter and sugar. Mix with an electric mixer on medium for approximately 3 minutes until fluffy.
5. Scrape down the sides of the bowl. Add in the egg and vanilla. Mix until completely combined.
6. Scrape down the sides of the bowl for a second time. Add in the egg yolk. Mix until completely combined.
7. Set the mixer to low. While continuing to mix, add in half of the flour mixture (from step 3), then the milk and then remaining flour mixture.
8. Grease a 9 x 13″ (20 x 30cm) baking tin, then line with parchment paper. Butter the parchment.
9. Pour the mixture into the tin to create a thin layer. Use the back of a spatula to smooth into an even layer.
10. Bake for approximately 12 minutes. When ready, it will be golden brown and springy when lightly touched.
11. Allow the cake tin to cool for 10 minutes on a cooling rack.
12. Slide a small knife around the cake. Then remove the cake from the tin and place upside down on a cooling rack until fully cooled.
13. Once fully cooled, divide the cake into thirds. You want 3 rectangles that measure 9 x 4⅓″ (23 x 11cm) each.

To prepare the cream filling

1. In a large bowl, add in the cream. Mix with an electric mixer until stiff peaks form. Set aside.
2. In a separate bowl, add in the peaches (from the earlier fruits preparation step), evaporated milk, peach preserves, and salt.
3. Gently fold in the cream (from step 1).

To assemble the cake

1. Line a 9 x 5″ (23 x 13cm) loaf tin with plastic wrap. Ensure there is a 7″ (18cm) overhang on both sides.
2. Ensure that the three cake layers fit in the tin. You may need to cut them to fit. Ideally, once the cake is in the tin, there should be a ¼″ (0.6cm) gap between the cake and the edges of the tin. Once you have ensured the cake layers fit, remove them from the tin.
3. Add a third of the cream filling mixture into the tin. Use the back of a spatula to smooth into an even layer.
4. Place one of the cake layers on top. Gently press down to allow the cream to come up evenly around the sides of the cake.
5. Take the raspberries (from the earlier fruits preparation step) and drain them. Divide them into two halves and spread one half on top of the cake layer.
6. Repeat steps 3 to 5 to create further layers of cream filling, cake, and raspberries.
7. On the new second layer of raspberries, place all the remaining cream filling. Then place the final cake layer on top. As before, gently press down to allow the cream filling to come up evenly around the sides of the cake.
8. Pull up the plastic wrap overhang from the sides to tightly wrap the cake.
9. Freeze for approximately 9 hours. When ready, the cake will become firm.

To finish the cake

1. Remove the cake from freezer.
2. Remove the plastic wrapping and then remove cake from tin.

3. Place upside down on plate. Allow to reach room temperature.
4. Thinly slice the peach.
5. In a separate bowl, add in the peach, raspberries, and sugar.
6. Gently stir, then allow the mixture to stand for 10 minutes.
7. Spread the mixture on top of the cake.

Shopping list

Purchase specialty ingredients on Amazon:

Raspberries	http://amzn.to/2lALn1D
Evaporated milk	http://amzn.to/2HNzt35
Peach preserves	http://amzn.to/2G2GUX4

Nutritional information (per serving)

Calories	288	
Total Fat	13g	(daily value 17%)
Saturated Fat	7.7g	(daily value 39%)
Trans Fat	0g	
Cholesterol	61mg	(daily value 20%)
Sodium	137mg	(daily value 6%)
Potassium	231mg	(daily value 5%)
Total Carb	41g	(daily value 15%)
Dietary Fiber	3.3g	(daily value 12%)
Sugars	28.4g	
Protein	4.2g	
Vitamin A	11%	
Vitamin C	17%	
Vitamin D	18mcg (92%)	
Calcium	80mg (6%)	
Iron	1mg (5%)	

Berry Meringue Ice Cream Cake

A lovely berry cake that won't fail to impress and is quick and easy to make!

Makes 12 servings.

Ingredients

For the base cake

8½ cups (2 quarts, 2 liters) vanilla ice cream
2 cups (500g) mixed berries
100g packet of meringues, crushed (a 100g packet will usually have 8 meringues).

For the finishing

Chocolate suitable for grating*
2 cups (500g) mixed berries
Confectioners' sugar for dusting*

Vary amount according to preference.

Steps

To prepare the base cake

1. In a large bowl, add in the ice cream. Allow to stand for 10 minutes, until the ice cream begins to soften.
2. Add in berries and meringue. Stir until combined.
3. Grease a 9″ (23cm) round springform tin. Line both the base and sides with baking paper.
4. Pour the mixture into the tin. Use the back of a spatula to create a smooth and even layer.
5. Cover with plastic wrap.
6. Freeze for 8 hours until firm.

To finish the cake

1. Remove cake from tin.
2. Grate the chocolate over the top of the cake.
3. Decorate with mixed berries.
4. Dust with confectioners' sugar. Serve immediately.

Shopping list

Purchase specialty ingredients on Amazon:

Vanilla ice cream	http://amzn.to/2G6nrEN
Mixed berries	http://amzn.to/2G8kuUi
Meringues	http://amzn.to/2Glu7qD

Nutritional information (per serving)

Calories	87	
Total Fat	1.3g	(daily value 2%)
Saturated Fat	0.8g	(daily value 4%)
Trans Fat	0.3g	
Cholesterol	5mg	(daily value 2%)
Sodium	36mg	(daily value 2%)
Potassium	75mg	(daily value 2%)
Total Carb	17.7g	(daily value 6%)
Dietary Fiber	1.6g	(daily value 6%)
Sugars	15.3g	
Protein	1.4g	
Vitamin A	4%	
Vitamin C	6%	
Vitamin D	0mcg (0%)	
Calcium	19mg (1%)	
Iron	0mg (3%)	

Almond & Strawberry Ice Cream Cake

A wonderful cake bursting with natural flavors!

Makes 8 servings.

Ingredients

For the base cake
½ cup (110g) unsalted butter
¾ cup (150g) sugar
3 large (171g) eggs
1 cup (100g) cake flour
½ tsp (2.40g) baking powder
2 tbsp (13g) dry powdered milk
1 tbsp (15ml) corn syrup
Juice of half a small lemon (approx. 1½ tbsp, 25ml)
¼ tsp (1.4g) allspice
¼ tsp (1.4g) nutmeg
¼ tsp (6.00g) salt
½ vanilla bean

For the whipped cream filling
1 cup (240g) heavy whipping cream
1 tbsp (12g) sugar
1 vanilla bean

For the cake assembly
2 cups (½ quart, ½ liter) strawberry ice cream
10 whole strawberries (approx. 96g)
½ cup (60g) crushed almonds

Steps

To prepare the base cake
1. Leave the butter out at room temperature to allow it to soften.
2. Preheat oven to 325°F (180°C).
3. In a bowl, add in the butter and sugar. Using an electric mixer, beat until fluffy.
4. Add in eggs one at a time and mix well after each.
5. Add in cake flour, baking powder, powdered milk, and corn syrup, mixing well after each.
6. Add in the lemon juice, allspice, nutmeg, salt, and vanilla. Mix until completely combined.
7. Grease a 9 x 5″ (23 x 13cm) loaf tin and pour batter in.
8. Bake for approximately 45 minutes.
9. When ready, you can place a knife in the center and it will come out clean.
10. Allow the cake tin to cool for 10 minutes on a cooling rack.
11. Remove the cake from the tin and place on a cooling rack until fully cooled.
12. Once cooled, cut into 8 slices.

To prepare the whipped cream filling
1. In a bowl, add in the cream, sugar, and vanilla.
2. Using a mixer, beat on high for approximately 3 minutes until stiff peaks form.
3. Set aside and keep refrigerated.

To assemble the cake
1. Line a 9 x 5″ (23 x 13cm) loaf tin with aluminum foil. Ensure there is an overhang on both sides.
2. Place 4 of the cake slices into the tin.
3. Slice the strawberries and then divide the whipped cream into two halves.
4. Now create the following layers: ice cream, strawberries, first half of whipped cream, 4 remaining cake slices, second half of whipped cream. Ensure each layer is smooth.
5. Sprinkle the crushed almonds on top.
6. Place in freezer for 8 hours.

7. When ready, lift the cake out of the tin using the overhanging foil to help.
8. Slice and serve immediately.

Nutritional information (per serving)

Calories	416	
Total Fat	28.3g	(daily value 36%)
Saturated Fat	15.1g	(daily value 75%)
Trans Fat	0.1g	
Cholesterol	134mg	(daily value 45%)
Sodium	200mg	(daily value 9%)
Potassium	180mg	(daily value 5%)
Total Carb	37.1g	(daily value 14%)
Dietary Fiber	1.6g	(daily value 6%)
Sugars	23.5g	
Protein	6.5g	
Vitamin A	4%	
Vitamin C	0%	
Vitamin D	29mcg (145%)	
Calcium	94mg (7%)	
Iron	1mg (7%)	

Malted Vanilla Ice Cream Cake

The frosting is made from malted milk and so has a wonderfully white appearance that resembles a winter wonderland. And the taste is just as enchanting, with a delicate sweetness that is simply tantalizing!

Makes 12 servings.

Ingredients

For the base angel food cake
1¾ cups (350g) sugar
1 cup (100g) cake flour
¼ tsp (1.5g) salt
12 regular (360ml) egg whites
6 tsp (35ml) lemon juice
1 tsp (6ml) juice squeezed from an orange
⅓ cup (70ml) warm water

For the frosting
½ cup (120ml) heavy cream
¼ cup (25g) malted milk powder
6 cups (1½ quarts, 1.5 liters) vanilla ice cream

For the finishing
Additional 1 cup (240ml) heavy cream
Additional 2 tbsp (10g) malted milk powder
Handful of white sprinkles

Steps

To prepare the base angel food cake

1. Preheat oven to 350°F (180°C).
2. In a food processor, add in the sugar. Blend for approximately 2 minutes until superfine.
3. Divide the sugar into two halves. Set aside one half.
4. In a bowl, add in one half of the sugar, cake flour, and salt. Mix and sift to remove all lumps. Set aside.
5. In a separate large bowl, add in the egg whites, lemon juice, orange juice, and water. Whisk until completely combined.
6. After 2 minutes, use an electric whisk on medium speed. While continuing to mix, slowly sift in the remaining half of the sugar (from step 3).
7. Eventually medium sized peaks will form. Once this happens, slowly sift in the flour mixture (from step 4) to dust the top of the foam. Then use a spatula to gently fold in. Repeat this process until all the flour mixture is used.
8. Slowly place the mixture into a tube tin (that has not been greased), one spoon at a time. When finished, use the back of a spatula to spread out evenly and smooth.
9. Bake for approximately 35 minutes. When ready, you can insert a wooden skewer halfway between the inner and outer walls, and the skewer will come out dry.
10. Turn the cake upside down onto a cooling rack and allow to stand for at least an hour.
11. Remove from tin.

To prepare the frosting

1. Leave the cream out at room temperature for 10 to 15 minutes to allow it to soften.
2. In a bowl, add in the heavy cream and malted milk powder. Mix until the milk powder is mostly dissolved.
3. Allow to sit for 5 minutes.
4. Mix again and continue mixing until the milk powder is completely dissolved. The mixture should be slightly thickened. Set aside.
5. Using a serrated knife, cut the brown crust off the top, bottom, and sides of the angel food cake.

6. Cut the cake into thin slices.
7. Take a 10 x 4" (25 x 10cm) tube pan and gently coat the bottom and sides with cooking spray.
8. Take half the cake slices and press on the bottom of the tin. They should also be slightly pressed against the sides of the tin, trimming any excess. The goal is to create a single layer.
9. Drizzle half of the cream mixture (from step 4) on the cake slices.
10. In the tin, add in half the ice cream. Use the back of a spatula to flatten the ice cream into an even layer.
11. Press some of the remaining cake slices on the ice cream layer to make an additional layer. Trim as necessary to ensure this layer is even.
12. Drizzle the remaining cream over the cake layer to create an additional new layer.
13. Use the remaining ice cream and cake slices to create new layers.
14. Cover with plastic wrap and freeze for 5 hours until firm.
15. Use a spatula to loosen the edges of the cake, then turn upside down.

To finish the cake

1. In a bowl, add in the heavy cream and malted milk powder. Mix with an electric mixer until stiff peaks form.
2. Spread the mixture onto the top and sides of the cake.
3. Decorate with white sprinkles.

Storage

The cake can remain frozen for 5 days.

Shopping list

Purchase specialty ingredients on Amazon:

Malted milk powder   http://amzn.to/2FNGJ2w

White sprinkles   http://amzn.to/2G7NDPC

Nutritional information (per serving)

Calories	352	
Total Fat	19.9g	(daily value 26%)
Saturated Fat	12.3g	(daily value 62%)
Trans Fat	0g	
Cholesterol	73mg	(daily value 24%)
Sodium	112mg	(daily value 5%)
Potassium	126mg	(daily value 3%)
Total Carb	39.6g	(daily value 14%)
Dietary Fiber	0.3g	(daily value 1%)
Sugars	31.5g	
Protein	5.9g	
Vitamin A	5%	
Vitamin C	2%	
Vitamin D	26mcg (132%)	
Calcium	50mg (4%)	
Iron	0mg (3%)	

Salty Peanut & Pretzel Ice Cream Cake

A unique savory and sweet taste explosion made from delicious gooey peanut butter and cream together with crunchy, salty pretzels and peanuts.

Makes 10 servings.

Ingredients

For the crust and crumbly topping
¼ cup (55g) unsalted butter
2 tbsp (25g) light brown sugar
¼ cup (35g) dry-roasted salted peanuts
2 cups (90g) mini pretzels

For the filling
¾ cup (200g) unsweetened peanut butter
8 cups (2 quarts, 2 liters) high-quality vanilla ice cream

For the assembly
2 tbsp (42g) honey

For the finishing
1 cup (240ml) heavy cream
2 tbsp (20g) dry-roasted salted peanuts

Steps

To prepare the crust and crumbly topping
1. Preheat oven to 350°F (180°C).
2. In a medium saucepan, add in the butter. Cook on medium heat until melted. Allow to fully cool.

3. In a food processor, add in the brown sugar, peanuts, and pretzels.
4. Blend the mixture so it becomes coarse with only a few large bits.
5. Add in the butter. Blend until completely combined.
6. Take ¼ cup of the mixture. Spread it on a half sheet pan (rimmed baking sheet). Take care to form an even layer. This will form the crumbly topping.
7. Take the remaining three-quarter cup of the mixture and place on the base of a 9″ (23cm) springform tin. Press the mixture down to create a firm layer. This will form the crust.
8. Bake both the crust tin and crumbs sheet until light and golden brown. This will take approximately 8 minutes for the crust and 5 minutes for the crumbs.
9. Allow both items to cool completely on a cooling rack.

To prepare the filling
1. Stir the peanut butter well to remove all lumps. Set aside.
2. Divide the ice cream into two halves.
3. Place one half into a large bowl and break into pieces.
4. Allow to sit at room temperature for approximately 10 minutes so it softens.
5. Gently fold in the peanut butter (from step 1). Set aside.

To assemble the cake
1. Place the ice cream and peanut butter mixture onto the crust (while keeping the crust in the tin) and use the back of a spatula to spread it evenly over the crust. Use gentle movements to avoid pulling the crust out of the tin.
2. Drizzle the first tablespoon of honey on top.
3. Sprinkle ½ cup of the cooled crumbs on top. Gently press them into the ice cream.
4. Cover the tin with plastic wrap and then place in freezer for approximately 1 hour.
5. Take the second half of the ice cream and prepare with the peanut butter as before (see filling preparation).
6. Remove cake from freezer and then repeat steps 1 and 2, to create a second layer of filling and honey.
7. Cover the tin with plastic wrap.

8. Place in freezer for 5 hours. Do not leave for longer than 8 hours as it will become too hard.

To finish the cake
1. In a bowl, add in the cream. Whip until soft peaks form.
2. Add in the peanuts and remaining crumbs. Mix until combined. Set aside.
3. Remove the cake from the freezer.
4. Dip a large knife into boiling water. Run around the inside edge of the cake tin to loosen the cake.
5. Remove the outer edge ring of the cake tin.
6. Gently spread the cream mixture (from step 2) on top.
7. Serve immediately.

Shopping list

Purchase specialty ingredients on Amazon:

Mini pretzels	http://amzn.to/2FOlbC0
Unsweetened peanut butter	http://amzn.to/2G4BMBY
Dry-roasted salted peanuts	http://amzn.to/2G74r9u
Vanilla ice cream	http://amzn.to/2IxNJ1g

Nutritional information (per serving)

Calories	366	
Total Fat	28.9g	(daily value 37%)
Saturated Fat	11.9g	(daily value 60%)
Trans Fat	0.076g	
Cholesterol	51mg	(daily value 17%)
Sodium	265mg	(daily value 12%)
Potassium	51mg	(daily value 5%)
Total Carb	22g	(daily value 8%)
Dietary Fiber	2.5g	(daily value 9%)
Sugars	10.1g	
Protein	7.3g	
Vitamin A	8%	
Vitamin C	0%	
Vitamin D	16mcg (79%)	
Calcium	35mg (3%)	
Iron	1mg (4%)	

Chocolate & Coconut Sorbet Baked Alaska

This cake seems magical, as the ice cream stays unmelted despite being baked inside a warm cake! A coconut sorbet is incorporated to add a fantastically wonderful twist!

Makes 12 servings.

Ingredients

For the coconut sorbet
3¾ cups (27oz, 800ml) coconut milk
2 cups (15oz, 450ml) cream of coconut
½ cup (30g) sweetened flaked coconut
1½ cups (350ml) water

For the chocolate ice cream
⅔ cup (115g) semisweet chocolate
3 large (45ml) egg yolks
½ cup (100g) sugar
2 cups (475ml) heavy cream
2 cups (470ml) milk
2 vanilla beans

For the base sponge cake
1½ cups (190g) all-purpose flour
4 regular (120ml) egg whites
4 tbsp (50g) sugar
3 large (45ml) egg yolks
Additional 2 tbsp (25g) sugar
1 vanilla bean

For meringue for the Baked Alaska
4 regular (120ml) egg whites
¼ cup (50g) sugar

Steps

This recipe is made up of various stages. At the core is the coconut sorbet and chocolate ice cream. These are wrapped inside a sponge cake, which is placed to set in a bombe mold. The whole item is then decorated with a meringue to form the Baked Alaska.

To prepare the coconut sorbet

1. In a food processor, add in the coconut milk and cream of coconut. Blend for 1 minute until smooth.
2. Pour into a bowl and add in the flaked coconut and water. Refrigerate for 4 hours until very cold.
3. If you have an ice cream maker, pour the mixture in and follow manufacturer's instructions. Transfer to freezer and freeze until firm. If you don't have an ice cream maker, then freeze the mixture until frozen, stirring vigorously every 30 minutes, taking care to break up any frozen clumps (It should take about 3 hours to complete).

To prepare the chocolate ice cream

1. Fill a large saucepan with water. Cook on medium heat.
2. Into the pan, place a smaller Pyrex or stainless steel bowl.
3. Place the chocolate in the smaller bowl, stirring occasionally to allow the chocolate to melt. Take care to ensure that the base does not scorch and that the steam from the bottom pan doesn't enter the bowl with chocolate (You can also use a double boiler instead of the two pans). Once ready, set aside.
4. In a separate bowl, add in the egg yolks and the sugar. Whisk until creamy and smooth. Set aside.
5. In a separate saucepan, add in the heavy cream, milk, and vanilla. Cook on medium heat and bring to a boil. Then lower the heat and allow to simmer.
6. Pour one-third of the hot milk mixture into the egg mixture (from step 4). Stir until completely combined.
7. Now take the combined mixture and pour into the remaining hot milk mixture. While pouring, use a wire whisk to stir.
8. Continue to stir but now with a wooden spoon. Keep stirring until it becomes thick enough to coat the back side of the spoon.

9. Pour in the chocolate (from step 3), again using a wire whisk to stir while pouring.
10. Pour the mixture through a fine-mesh strainer over a container.
11. Fill a large bowl with ice and water. Then place the container in it (from step 10) to allow it to cool evenly.
12. Refrigerate for 8 hours then transfer to freezer.

To prepare the base sponge cake
1. Preheat the oven to 425°F (220°C).
2. In a bowl, add in the all-purpose flour. Mix to aerate and remove any lumps. Set aside.
3. In a separate bowl, add in the egg whites. Mix with an electric mixer until soft peaks form.
4. Add in the first 4 tbsp sugar and then continue mixing until the sugar mixes with the peaks. Set aside.
5. In a separate bowl, add in the egg yolks, the additional 2 tbsp sugar, and vanilla. Whisk until creamy and yellow.
6. Gently fold in the egg white mixture (from step 4).
7. Gently fold in the flour (from step 2).
8. Line a cookie sheet with parchment paper.
9. Pour the batter on the sheet. Use the back of a spatula to spread out evenly.
10. Bake for 15 minutes, until the top is golden brown. Begin checking after the first 10 minutes as it can burn quite quickly. For best results, place in the center of oven.
11. Remove tin from oven and place on a cooling rack until fully cooled.

To assemble the sponge cake with ice cream
1. Cut the cooled sponge cake to fit the bombe mold. To do this, cut into 2 pieces: a larger piece that will line the mold and a smaller piece for the top part of the mold (when the mold is inverted, this will become the base of the cake).
2. Line the bombe mold with plastic wrap. Place the large cake piece on the wrap.
3. Retrieve the sorbet and ice cream from the freezer. Leave to stand for 10 minutes to allow them to soften.
4. Spoon the sorbet into the mold to create an even layer over the existing layer of cake.

5. Spoon the ice cream onto the sorbet layer, again taking care to create an even layer.
6. Take the smaller sponge cake piece and place on top of the ice cream layer. It should seal the ice cream in.
7. Freeze for approximately 5 hours.(You can prepare this in advance, but don't keep it frozen for more than 2 weeks).

To make the meringue for the Baked Alaska

1. In a bowl, add in the egg whites. Mix with an electric mixer until soft peaks form.
2. Add in the sugar and then continue mixing until the sugar combines with the peaks. The peaks should be stiff (without becoming dry) to create the meringue.
3. Pour the meringue into a pastry bag that has a star tip.

To assemble the Baked Alaska

1. Preheat the oven to 450°F (230°C).
2. Remove the sponge cake from the bombe mold. If it has trouble coming out, place hot towels over it. It should now be upside down on a plate. Remove the plastic wrap.
3. Use the meringue pastry bag to decorate the base of the bombe, then move on to cover the bombe in full. This will need to be done with speed to avoid melting the ice cream.
4. Bake for 5 minutes. The meringue should become lightly browned without melting the ice cream.
5. Remove from oven, slice, and serve immediately.

Shopping list

Purchase specialty ingredients on Amazon:

Coconut milk	http://amzn.to/2GaBMQC
Cream of coconut	http://amzn.to/2DCREGs
Sweetened flaked coconut	http://amzn.to/2prx0DZ
Semisweet chocolate	http://amzn.to/2ppUzNB

Nutritional information (per serving)

Calories	797	
Total Fat	64.9g	(daily value 83%)
Saturated Fat	48.4g	(daily value 242%)
Trans Fat	0.1g	
Cholesterol	206mg	(daily value 69%)
Sodium	96mg	(daily value 4%)
Potassium	368mg	(daily value 8%)
Total Carb	47.5g	(daily value 17%)
Dietary Fiber	3.1g	(daily value 11%)
Sugars	23.2g	
Protein	13.7g	
Vitamin A	0%	
Vitamin C	14%	
Vitamin D	35mcg (173%)	
Calcium	112mg (9%)	
Iron	3mg (18%)	

Shortbread Honeycomb Ice Cream Cake

A treasure to behold, this cake is decorated with shortbread ice cream sandwich stars which are simply irresistible!

Makes 12 servings.

Ingredients

For the base cake
½ cup (125g) butter
1 cup (125g) all-purpose flour
1½ tbsp (10g) cocoa powder
2 tbsp (20g) rice flour
½ cup (60g) confectioners' sugar
1 vanilla bean
2 tsp (35ml) milk

For the ice cream filling
13 cups (3 quarts, 3 liters) vanilla ice cream
2½ cups (400g) chopped chocolate honeycomb pieces (approx. 1 packet)
Additional 6 cups (1¾ quart, 1.5 liters) vanilla ice cream

For the finishing
1 cup (160g) chocolate
½ cup (100g) coconut oil
1 cup (190g) sliced apricot pieces

Steps

To prepare the base cake and stars
1. Leave the butter out at room temperature to allow it to soften.

2. Preheat oven to 300°F (150°C).
3. In a bowl, add in the all-purpose flour, cocoa powder, and rice flour. Mix to aerate and remove any lumps. Set aside.
4. In a separate bowl, add in the butter, confectioners' sugar, and vanilla. Use an electric mixer to mix for approximately 5 minutes until fluffy.
5. Add in the milk and flour mixture (from step 3).
6. Mix on low speed until just combined.
7. Lightly flour a chopping board. Then gently knead the mixture on the board until it forms a dough.
8. Divide the dough into two halves. Cover the first half in plastic wrap and refrigerate for 45 minutes or until firm.
9. Grease a 9″ (23cm) springform tin. Line base and sides with baking paper. Ensure there is a 1″ (2.5cm) overhang on both sides.
10. Take the second dough half and roll it between 2 sheets of baking paper. You want to make a round shape that will fit in the springform tin.
11. Carefully place the round shape onto the springform tin. It should cover the base. Gently press it down to remove air bubbles.
12. Place the tin on a baking tray. Bake for 30 minutes. When ready, it will be firm to touch.
13. Allow the tin to completely cool.
14. Remove the first dough half (from step 8) from the fridge.
15. Place between two sheets of baking paper and roll to make it 0.1″ (3 mm) thick.
16. Use a star-shape cutter to cut 20 stars. A 2.75″ (6cm) cutter works best. You can combine and flatten any leftover dough scraps to make more stars.
17. Line 2 large baking trays with baking paper. Place stars onto tray. Leave a ⅓″ (0.7cm) gap between each star.
18. Bake for 6 minutes, swap trays (so the bottom tray moves to the top of the oven and vice-versa) and then bake for a further 6 minutes (12 minutes in total). When ready, the stars will be firm to touch.
19. Allow the trays to cool for 3 minutes.
20. Remove stars from trays and place on a cooling rack until fully cooled. If not using immediately, store in an airtight container.

To prepare ice cream filling and ice cream cake

1. In a bowl, add in the first (13 cups) portion of ice cream. Allow to stand for 10 minutes to soften (without melting).
2. Add in three-quarters of the honeycomb. Fold until combined.
3. Take the prepared base (from the earlier base cake preparation) and spread the ice cream over the top. Use the back of a spatula to create a smooth and even layer. Freeze for 8 hours.
4. In a separate bowl, place the additional ice cream. As before, allow to stand for 10 minutes to soften (without melting).
5. Add in the remaining honeycomb pieces. Fold until combined.
6. Grease a 13 x 10″ (30 x 19cm) Lamington tin, then line with baking paper. Ensure there is a 1″ (2.5cm) overhang on both sides. Spread the mixture into the tin, again using the back of a spatula to create a smooth and even layer. Freeze for 8 hours.

To assemble the cake stars

1. Remove the ice cream Lamington tin from freezer and allow to stand for 3 minutes.
2. Cut stars from ice cream, using a star cutter to create 10 stars.
3. Place the ice cream stars in between the shortbread ones. You should end up with 10 star sandwiches consisting of a shortbread top and bottom and an ice cream middle. Arrange them on a tray and keep in the freezer.

To finish the cake

1. Remove ice cream cake from freezer and then from the tin.
2. In a saucepan, add in the chocolate and coconut oil. Gently warm on medium heat until it is fully melted.
3. Remove from heat. Thoroughly stir to ensure that there are no lumps.
4. Allow to cool for a few seconds. Once it cools, it will become hard, so do not let it cool for too long!
5. Pour the sauce over the cake. Within a few seconds, the sauce will cool and become hard, forming a shell-like structure.

6.   Immediately place the sandwiches and apricot pieces on top
     so they stick to the cake. Dust with confectioners' sugar.
     Serve immediately.

Shopping list

Purchase specialty ingredients on Amazon:

Rice flour	http://amzn.to/2GGZLoz
Vanilla ice cream	http://amzn.to/2IxNJ1g
Chocolate	http://amzn.to/2FOJqRG
Coconut oil	http://amzn.to/2ppw9DJ
Apricot	http://amzn.to/2ppIKXM

Nutritional information (per serving)

Calories	339	
Total Fat	23.8g	(daily value 30%)
Saturated Fat	17.2g	(daily value 86%)
Trans Fat	0.327g	
Cholesterol	37mg	(daily value 12%)
Sodium	92mg	(daily value 4%)
Potassium	177mg	(daily value 4%)
Total Carb	29.3g	(daily value 11%)
Dietary Fiber	1.5g	(daily value 5%)
Sugars	13.7g	
Protein	3.6g	
Vitamin A	1%	
Vitamin C	3%	
Vitamin D	6mcg (29%)	
Calcium	66mg (5%)	
Iron	1mg (6%)	

Almond, Cherry & Chocolate Cookie Ice Cream Cake

A wonderful mixture of different flavors with almonds, cherries, chocolate, and cookies, all combining to make an irresistible cake!

Makes 8 servings.

Ingredients

For the base cake
6 cups (1½ quart, 1.4 liters) vanilla ice cream
2 cups (450g) fresh cherries
⅓ cup (70ml) water
1 packet (250g) chocolate cookies
¼ cup (50g) butter
1 cup (80g) chopped almonds

For the finishing
¼ cup (20g) slivered almonds

Steps

To prepare the base cake
1. Leave the ice cream out at room temperature for 20 to 25 minutes to allow it to soften.
2. Remove stones from cherries. In a saucepan over high heat, fill with water and add in cherries.
3. When boiling, reduce to medium heat then simmer for 12 minutes. Allow to cool. Set aside.
4. In a food processor, add in the chocolate cookies. Blend until fine like breadcrumbs. Set aside.
5. In a saucepan on medium heat, add in the butter and gently melt.

6. In a large bowl, add in the cookie crumbs (from step 4) and melted butter. Mix until completely combined.
7. Gently brush a springform cake tin with cooking oil.
8. Spoon the mixture into the tin, taking care to press it down firmly on the base. Use the back of a spatula to create a smooth and even layer.
9. In a bowl, add in the ice cream, the almonds, and three-quarters of the cherries (from step 3). Mix until completely combined. Pour into cake tin. Again, smooth down to create an even layer.
10. Cover tin with cling wrap. Freeze for 2 hours.
11. Remove from freezer and add remaining cherries. Return to freezer for a further hour.

To serve and finish the cake

1. Remove from freezer 10 minutes before serving.
2. Gently remove the cake from tin. If necessary, you can stand tin in a bowl of shallow water to allow it to loosen provided the tin is watertight.
3. Once removed, use a spatula to smooth outsides.
4. Sprinkle slivered almonds on top.

Shopping list

Purchase specialty ingredients on Amazon:

Cherries	http://amzn.to/2G64Pow
Vanilla ice cream	http://amzn.to/2IxNJ1g
Almonds	http://amzn.to/2FNIqwU
Chocolate cookies	http://amzn.to/2G79x5u

Nutritional information (per serving)

Calories	327	
Total Fat	15.8g	(daily value 20%)
Saturated Fat	5.7g	(daily value 29%)
Trans Fat	0.244g	
Cholesterol	19mg	(daily value 6%)
Sodium	237mg	(daily value 10%)
Potassium	223mg	(daily value 5%)
Total Carb	43.3g	(daily value 16%)
Dietary Fiber	2.7g	(daily value 10%)
Sugars	12.1g	
Protein	4.8g	
Vitamin A	2%	
Vitamin C	19%	
Vitamin D	4mcg (18%)	
Calcium	59mg (5%)	
Iron	2mg (10%)	

Youth Spell Cake

This next recipe is just for fun!

All the recipes in this book were featured in the cozy mystery story *Fairy Cake Fatality*. The story revolves around Faye Anderson, who discovers that she is a fairy that can cast magic spells by baking cakes! One of the recipes in the story is a Youth Spell cake. The recipe is included here, but of course, it's just for fun. You would need to be a fairy in order to bake it for real!

Learn more about the book here:
http://bit.ly/fairycake3
(More info about the book is after this recipe)

****

Youth Spell Cake Recipe

From *The Fairy Book of Spells*, this magic cake can make you younger.

Makes 1 cake with 0 servings (as it shouldn't be eaten).

Ingredients

8 large (456g) eggs
2 cups (220g) unsalted butter
15 cups (2500g) all-purpose flour
5 cups (625g) milk
8 cups (1600g) salt
3 cups (580g) leaves
½ cup (120ml) jasmine oil
2 daisy flowers
1 spider's web
19 cups (120g) brown sugar

Steps

1. Leave the butter and eggs out so they reach room temperature and the butter is softened.
2. Preheat oven to 350°F (180°C).
3. In a bowl, add in the all-purpose flour and salt. Whisk to aerate it and remove any lumps. Set aside.
4. In a food processor, blend the leaves into a purée. Set aside.
5. In a separate bowl, add in the daisy flowers, spider's web, and milk. Allow to stand for at least 10 minutes. Set aside.
6. In a large saucepan, add in the butter. Cook on low heat until the butter begins to melt. The butter should become soft without changing color or completely losing its structure.
7. Pour the butter into a large bowl and whisk thoroughly. It should become completely liquid.
8. Crack the eggs and separate the whites.
9. Add in the egg whites to the bowl with the butter. Whisk the egg whites at high speed. When ready, stiff peaks will form.
10. Add in the flour mixture (from step 3). Whisk until completely combined.
11. Add in the brown sugar. Whisk until completely combined.
12. Add in the puréed leaves (from step 4) and the jasmine oil. Whisk until completely combined.
13. Add in the daisy and spider's web milk (from step 5).
14. A fairy must use his or her finger to stir the mixture 3 times. Non-fairies can substitute this step by adding a pinch of fairy magic.
15. Grease a round 6″ (15cm) cake tin, then line with baking paper.
16. Pour the mixture into the cake tin. The cake tin should be ¾ full.
17. Bake for 30 minutes.

Magical information

Linkles	0.31 fg
Plinks	0.52 fg
Sparkles	1.1 sk
Magical Grade	A

Fairy Cake Faker
**Fairy cakes, a kitten, magic, and a murder to prevent in England
...all with a fairy twist!**

(The Cake Fairy Mysteries – Book 3)

Things should finally be going well for Faye Anderson. After all, her struggling cake shop is starting to make a profit. Her life, at last, seems to be in balance.

Except her pet cat Tom keeps on having nightmares that suggest something terrible is about to occur.

And when Faye finds the body of a dear friend, she realizes that more murders are about to hit the sleepy town of Fairfields.

It's going to be a tricky case to solve, especially since there doesn't seem to be any clues. Can Faye find the culprit before disaster strikes?

***Learn more*:**
http://bit.ly/fairycake3

3 FREE Bonus Ice Cream Recipes + FREE Future Books

Join my VIP club to get:

1) FREE Cookbook
Ice Cream Magic contains these three bonus ice cream recipes:

BONUS 1: Cake Batter Ice Cream

BONUS 2: Pumpkin Ice Cream

BONUS 3: Lavender Honey Ice Cream

All ice creams can be made at home without the need for an ice cream maker.

2) FREE future books
Selected readers can get some of my future books for free.

3) Discounts and special offers
Get my future books at discounted prices (or even for free).

Use this link to join the club and receive your FREE copy:

http://bit.ly/icecreambook

My club is completely free.

Join my Facebook recipe group!

My Facebook group is a great place to:
- Hang out with other cookbook readers
- Get reading suggestions for other authors
- Get special offers on my books.

My group will be launching later in the year, but you can use this exclusive link to join now and be a **VIP member**:

Join now:
http://bit.ly/recipe-group

(My group is completely free.)

Check out my other dessert books

Baking Magic: The best cakes, cookies, and desserts recipes

• The very best recipes
• Step-by-step instructions
• Mouthwatering dishes, such as Chocolate Mousse Crêpes Cake, Pink Swirls Ombré Cake, Peppermint Truffles, and Giant Pizza Cookies!

Weave baking magic!

Learn more:
http://bit.ly/bakingmagicbook

Hawaiian Baking: Baking Magic 2

• The very best Hawaiian desserts recipes
• Step-by-step instructions
• Mouthwatering dishes, such as Chantilly Chocolate Chiffon Cake, Mango and Macadamia Hawaiian Cookies, Haupia and Chocolate Pie, Green Tea Fairy Cakes, and Chantilly Red Bean Paste Pancakes!

Learn more:
bit.ly/bakingmagicbook2

Low Carb Desserts

- ZERO Sweeteners
- Limited Edition Gift!
- Full Carb & Cal Counts

Make delicious low carb desserts without harmful sweeteners.

Learn more:
http://bit.ly/lowcarbbook

Check out my dessert mystery books

A collection of cozy cat mysteries that feature all the desserts from my recipe books.

Fairy Cake Fatality
Fairy cakes, a kitten, magic, and a murder in England ...all with a fairy twist!

(The Cake Fairy Mysteries – Book 1)

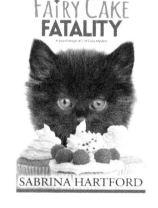

Faye left California to start a new life in England. Things aren't going well and her new cake shop is close to bankruptcy, but she gets a lucky break when she is chosen to be featured on the town's popular radio program. Unfortunately, on the day of the recording, a murder occurs and she is the prime suspect!

She tries to solve the case herself, but each clue she finds leaves her more confused. To make things worse, she keeps having hallucinations about being a fairy, but these only occur when a certain kitten is around. Or maybe there is something to these visions? Can Faye befriend the kitten and master her fairy past while solving the case?

Learn more:
http://bit.ly/fairycake1

Fairy Cake Betrayal
Fairy cakes, a kitten, magic, and an impossible murder in Hawaii ...all with a fairy twist!

(The Cake Fairy Mysteries – Book 2)

Faye Anderson is searching for her mother, who mysteriously disappeared over a decade ago. The quest takes Faye to Hawaii, where she stumbles upon a shadowy killer fleeing a murder scene. Unfortunately, the killer seems to be none other than her own mother. Worse still, when the police arrive, there don't seem to be any signs that a murder has taken place. There are no witnesses, and even the body is missing!

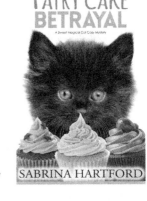

It's an impossible case, but Faye isn't going to let that stop her, especially when she can draw on her fairy powers, as well as the help of Tom, her newly adopted pet cat. But the island of Hawaii holds many unwanted secrets, such as the story behind her mom's disappearance and the truth about Tom's past. Solving the crime could lead to the ultimate betrayal...

Learn more:
http://bit.ly/fairycake2

Fairy Cake Faker
Fairy cakes, a kitten, magic, and a murder to prevent in England ...all with a fairy twist!

(The Cake Fairy Mysteries – Book 3)

Things should finally be going well for Faye Anderson. After all, her struggling cake shop is starting to make a profit. Her life, at last, seems to be in balance.

Except her pet cat Tom keeps on having nightmares that suggest something terrible is about to occur.

And when Faye finds the body of a dear friend, she realizes that more murders are about to hit the sleepy town of Fairfields.

It's going to be a tricky case to solve, especially since there doesn't seem to be any clues. Can Faye find the culprit before disaster strikes?

Learn more:
http://bit.ly/fairycake3

Enjoy this book: Yes/No?
– Contact the author

If you enjoyed the book...

If you enjoyed this book, please leave a review on Amazon.

I am just a regular girl and so don't have the time or money to compete with established publishers. Posting a review would help me greatly!!

Please leave your review here:
http://bit.ly/bakingmagic3review

(You will be asked to sign in to your Amazon account.)

If you disliked the book...

I really want you to enjoy this book. So if you have any issues, please contact me (the author) directly, and I will fix your issue!

Email: sabrina.hartford.books@gmail.com

I will personally respond to your email as soon as possible. Your feedback will also be considered for future updates. These updates will be provided FREE of charge to all existing readers.

The Cake Fairy Store

A range of limited edition products based on The Cake Fairy series. This range is always being updated.
Visit http://bit.ly/cake-fairy-store for the latest.

Tom and cakes 3

Limited edition:
Available in a range of colors and sizes.

http://bit.ly/tom-cakes-3

Tom pokes in

Limited edition:
Available in a range of colors and sizes.

http://bit.ly/kitty-poke-shirt

Over 10 other designs available!
Visit http://bit.ly/cake-fairy-store for the latest.

Images subject to change. Please visit the links to view the actual product before purchase. Please contact me if you are unable to make a purchase (sabrina.hartford.books@gmail.com).

Freebies & Offers

Honey Bar
Free online discounts + Free Amazon vouchers!

When shopping online, the Honey bar automatically applies discounts to your purchases.

You also receive bonus points, which you can exchange for Amazon gift vouchers!

- Works on many online stores.

- Works in multiple countries, including the US and UK.

- COMPLETELY FREE – No credit card or subscription required.

Install for free when you use this special link:
http://joinhoney.com/ref/ut22e0

Read Kindle books for free

Kindle Unlimited lets you read the vast majority of Kindle books for a low monthly fee. You can try the service FREE for 30 days and cancel the trial without paying a penny.

Use this exclusive link:
http://bit.ly/free-ku

Two free audiobooks

Get two free audiobooks when you sign up for a free 30 day trial of Audible from Amazon.

- Choose 2 free books from over 2 million titles.

- Cancel 30-day free trial without paying a penny.

Use this exclusive link:
http://bit.ly/2-free-audio

About the author

Sabrina Hartford just loves cooking and has been making sweet treats since she was two years old. Seriously, her baby photos show her helping her mama in the kitchen!

She has had a variety of jobs in her time, but now, when she's not following her first love of writing, she enjoys baking, traveling, volunteering, and reading books.

Email: sabrina.hartford.books@gmail.com

Don't forget to leave a review!

If you enjoyed this book, please leave a review on Amazon. I am just a regular girl and so don't have the time or money to compete with established publishers. Posting a review would help me greatly!!

Please leave your review here:
http://bit.ly/bakingmagic3review

(You will be asked to sign in to your Amazon account.)

If you didn't like the book, please email me with your comments, as I'd be more than happy to fix or consider any issues you may have.

Email: sabrina.hartford.books@gmail.com

Copyright

Special thanks to Madhu Sharma Ltd in the help given to bring this book to market.

© 2018 Madhu Sharma Ltd

Baking with Ice Cream
Baking Magic 3: The best ice cream cakes, cookies and desserts recipes
– A Cake Fairy Cookbook

BM3-SE-17jul18

Made in United States
North Haven, CT
13 May 2022

19142317R00049